THE SELF-EMPLOYED GUIDE-BOOK

The beginners guide to start, manage and grow a successful and profitable small-scale business

PATIENCE JOHN

Copyright © 2024 by Patience John

All rights reserved

No part of this publication may be reproduced, distributed, or transmitted in any form or by any means, including photocopying, recording, or other electronic or mechanical methods, without the prior written permission of the publisher, except in the case of brief quotations embodied in critical reviews and certain other non-commercial uses permitted by copyright law.

This is not the work of fiction but names, characters, places, and incidents either are the product of the author's imagination or are used fictitiously. Any resemblance to actual persons, living or dead, events, or locales is entirely coincidental

TABLE OF CONTENT

INTRODUCTION 5
   Why Choose Self-Employment? 5
   Who is This Guide For? 6
   The Rewards and Challenges of Running Your Own Business 7

PART 1 8
   Laying the Foundation 8
      Identifying Your Business Idea 8
      2. Validating Your Business Idea 9
      3. Creating a Business Plan 10

PART 2 12
   Starting Your Business 12
      4. Registering Your Business 12
      5. Financing Your Business 14
      6. Building Your Brand and Online Presence 15

PART 3 18
   Managing and Scaling Your Business 18
      7. Managing Day-to-Day Operations 18
      Time Management for Business Owners .. 18
      8. Growing Your Client Base 20

9. Scaling Your Business	21
PART 4	23
Sustaining Long-Term Success	23
10. Financial Management and Profitability	23
12. Planning for the Future	26
CONCLUSION	28
Reflecting on Your Entrepreneurial Journey	28
Staying Motivated and Focused on Your Goals	29
You will appreciate this words from me	30
BONUS	31
DONE FOR YOU- 6 BUSINESS IDEAS AND PLANS FOR BEGINNERS	31

INTRODUCTION

Are you thinking about starting your own business but not sure where to begin? You're in the right place. Starting a business can seem like a huge leap, especially if you've never done it before. Maybe you have a great idea but need some guidance on how to turn it into a reality. Or perhaps you're not even sure what kind of business you want to start yet, that's completely okay.

In this guide, I'll Walk you through every step, from choosing the right idea to building and growing a profitable business. Whether you're just starting out or looking for a new direction, this guide is here to help you make smart decisions and avoid common mistakes.

Why Choose Self-Employment?

Have you ever dreamed of being your own boss? Self-employment isn't just about making money, it's about freedom. You decide when you work, how you work, and most importantly, what kind of impact you want to make. You'll have the power to shape your future instead of following someone else's vision.

Of course, it's not always easy. There will be challenges, but the rewards? Those can be life-changing. With the right plan in place, you can turn your passion into something that gives you both financial independence and personal satisfaction.

So, if you've been thinking about stepping out on your own, now's the time to learn how to do it right.

Who is This Guide For?

This guide is for you. It's written for people who are ready to start their first business, no matter their background. Maybe you're leaving a job you don't love, or you're just starting your career and want more control. Whatever your situation, if you're driven and ready to learn, this guide will help you get there.

Don't worry if you don't have any experience. You don't need to be an expert to start a business. You just need the right mindset, a clear plan, and the determination to make it work. This guide will give you that plan.

The Rewards and Challenges of Running Your Own Business

Let's be real: starting a business can be challenging. There will be long hours and some tough decisions. But here's the good news, you're not alone. With the right approach, you can handle the ups and downs and come out stronger on the other side.

Running your own business will teach you so much more than just how to make money. You'll become a better problem-solver, learn to manage your time, and build relationships that help your business grow. Every step you take, every challenge you overcome, will bring you closer to building something you can be proud of.

This guide is not just about showing you how to start, it's about giving you the confidence to succeed. Ready to take the next step? Let's go!

PART 1

Laying the Foundation

Starting your own business can feel like a big challenge, especially if you're new to the field. But don't worry! With the right approach and planning, you can set yourself up for success. In this section, we'll break down the first essential steps to help you lay a strong foundation for your small-scale business.

Identifying Your Business Idea

Before you can launch a business, you need a clear idea of what you'll offer. But how do you find that perfect business idea? Start by thinking about three things:

Your Skills: What are you good at? It doesn't have to be something fancy, sometimes the best businesses come from simple skills like cooking, organizing, or fixing things.

Your Passion: What are you excited about? Passion helps you stay motivated, especially when challenges arise.

Market Needs: This is the most important part, what do people need that they're willing to pay for? Look at gaps in the market or common problems people have, and think about how your skills can help solve them.

When all three of these areas overlap, you've found a solid business idea. If you're unsure, start small. Test the waters by talking to people, asking for feedback, or even trying a few small projects to see what sticks.

2. Validating Your Business Idea

Having a great idea is a good start, but you need to be sure there's a demand for it. This is where **market research** comes in. Market research sounds complicated, but it's simply learning more about your potential customers and competitors.

Understanding Your Target Audience: Who are your potential customers? What problems do they face, and how does your business solve those problems? Get clear on who you're serving, whether it's busy parents, local small businesses, or people looking for a specific product or service. Don't forget that your business should center on helping people and solving their solution instead focusing on simply making money off them.

Competitive Analysis: Check out what others in your field are doing. What do they offer, and how can you do it better or differently? This will help you understand your competition and carve out a unique space for yourself.

Next, you'll want to **test your idea**. Before diving headfirst, find a way to get feedback. For example, if you're planning to sell a product, create a simple version or prototype and offer it to a few people for free or at a discounted rate in exchange for honest feedback. This allows you to tweak and refine your idea before fully launching it.

3. Creating a Business Plan

A business plan is your roadmap. It doesn't need to be complicated, but it should help you stay organized and focused as you build your business. Here's what it should include:

Vision, Mission, and Goals: Think about the bigger picture. Why are you starting this business? What's your long-term vision? Your mission will be the 'why' behind your business, and your goals are the specific targets you want to hit, both in the short and long term.

Financial Planning: This might sound intimidating, but it's critical to figure out your costs and potential revenue. How much will it cost to start, and how much do you need to keep the business running? Estimate things like supplies, marketing, and any other expenses you expect. Then, consider how much you'll charge and how many sales you'll need to cover your costs and make a profit.

Setting Milestones: Breaking your goals down into smaller steps helps make them more manageable. Set key performance indicators (KPIs) that allow you to track your progress. For example, "Get 50 new customers in 3 months" is a clear, trackable goal.

By taking these foundational steps, you'll have a clearer path forward and the confidence to get started. Remember, the beginning stages of building a business are all about planning and testing. You don't have to have everything figured out right away, focus on small steps and learn as you go. The more prepared you are now; the smoother things will be when you officially launch your business! let's examine more about in the next part.

PART 2

Starting Your Business

4. Registering Your Business

Starting a business is exciting, but before you dive in, it's crucial to get your legal setup right. Think of this as laying the foundation for your business – it will save you a lot of hassle down the road.

Choosing the Right Business Structure:

Your first step is to decide what type of business you want to run. For a beginner, a sole proprietorship is often the simplest. It allows you to own the business completely, but you're also personally responsible for any debts. If you want to separate your personal assets from the business, consider an LLC (Limited Liability Company). It provides protection but is still straightforward to manage.

Legal Requirements and Permits:

Next, you'll need to ensure that your business complies with local laws. Depending on your business type, you may need licenses or permits. For example, if you're opening a food-related business, health permits will be required. Check with your local government or a business advisor to ensure you're on track.

Setting Up Tax and Accounting Systems:

Taxes might sound daunting, but getting organized early is key. Open a separate bank account for your business and consider using simple accounting software like QuickBooks or Wave. Keeping your business and personal finances separate will make tax season much easier. And don't forget, you may need to pay quarterly taxes, so stay on top of your earnings from the beginning.

5. Financing Your Business

One of the biggest hurdles new entrepreneurs face is money. But don't worry – you can start small and grow as you go. Let's look at some smart ways to get your business off the ground financially.

Bootstrapping: How to Start with Limited Capital:

Many successful businesses started with little money. Bootstrapping means using your personal savings or income from another job to fund your business. It's about being resourceful and minimizing expenses. For example, if you're starting a freelance service, you probably don't need an office right away – work from home until you can afford more.

Exploring Funding Options: Loans, Grants, and Investors:

If you need more capital to get started, there are options available. Small business loans from a bank or credit union can help, but make sure you have a solid business plan to show how you'll use the money. There are also grants available for specific industries or groups, such as women or minority-owned businesses. Crowdfunding is another avenue platforms like Kickstarter allow you to raise money directly from your audience in exchange for early access to your product.

Managing Your Cash Flow from Day One:

Once the business is up and running, managing cash flow becomes a top priority. Cash flow refers to the money coming in (revenue) and going out (expenses). Track every dollar and make sure you're not spending more than you're bringing in. This may sound simple, but many businesses fail due to poor cash management. Stay on top of it, and you'll be in a good position to grow.

6. Building Your Brand and Online Presence

Building a brand is more than just a logo – it's about how your business is perceived by the world. In today's digital age, having an online presence is essential.

Choosing a Business Name and Creating Your Brand Identity:

Your business name is the first thing customers see, so make it count! It should be memorable, easy to pronounce, and give an idea of what you offer. Once you've nailed down a name, think about your brand's personality. Are you fun and friendly, or serious and professional? Your colors, fonts, and logo should reflect this personality.

Establishing a Website and Social Media Presence:

In today's world, customers expect to find you online. At the very least, create a simple website that explains who you are, what you do, and how people can contact you. You don't need to be a web design expert – platforms like Wix or Squarespace make it easy to build a professional-looking site. Once your site is up, focus on building a presence on social media. Choose platforms that align with your target audience – for instance, Instagram or TikTok if you're targeting a younger crowd, LinkedIn for a more professional audience.

Basics of Digital Marketing: SEO, Content, and Email Marketing:

Now that your brand is online, you'll want people to find it. Start by learning the basics of SEO (Search Engine Optimization), which helps your website rank higher on search engines like Google. Write clear, helpful content that your audience is searching for, and don't forget to update your site regularly. Email marketing is another low-cost way to keep your customers engaged. Collect email addresses on your website and send regular newsletters or updates about your services or products.

By focusing on these key steps in starting your business, you'll build a strong foundation that will set you up for long-term success. Remember, starting small is fine – what matters is consistency, planning, and adaptability as your business grows.

The next part will talk more.

PART 3

Managing and Scaling Your Business

Once your business is up and running, the next major challenge is managing it effectively and preparing for growth. The day-to-day operations can be demanding, but with the right strategies and tools, you can keep things organized, maintain steady growth, and eventually scale your business. Let's walk through the key steps to make that happen.

7. Managing Day-to-Day Operations

Running a small business requires juggling several tasks at once. From dealing with customers to managing your inventory, it can get overwhelming if you don't have a system in place. Here's how you can manage your operations smoothly:

Time Management for Business Owners

Time is one of your most valuable resources. Create a daily schedule to prioritize important tasks. Set aside time for admin work, marketing, and customer service, and don't be afraid to delegate when necessary. Remember, it's not just about working hard, but working smart.

Essential Tools for Running a Small Business

Make use of tools that can save you time and effort. For example, accounting software like QuickBooks or Xero can help manage finances. Tools like Trello or Asana can help you track tasks and projects. The right tools will keep you organized and free up time for growth activities.

Handling Invoicing, Inventory, and Customer Relations

Keeping track of cash flow and inventory is crucial. Automate invoicing where possible and stay on top of payments to avoid cash shortages. For inventory, use tracking systems to prevent overstocking or running out of key items. Lastly, nurture customer relationships by responding promptly to inquiries and feedback. Happy customers are more likely to return and recommend your business to others.

8. Growing Your Client Base

Your business can't survive without customers, and growing your client base is essential for long-term success. Fortunately, there are plenty of cost-effective ways to reach more people and turn them into loyal clients.

Effective Marketing Strategies on a Budget

You don't need to spend a fortune on marketing to attract customers. Start by using free platforms like social media to promote your business. Instagram, Facebook, and even LinkedIn can be powerful tools for reaching potential clients. Focus on content that provides value—whether it's tips, tutorials, or behind-the-scenes looks at your business.

Networking and Building Business Relationships

Networking is an often-overlooked aspect of business development, but it can open doors to opportunities you may not find otherwise. Attend local events, join online forums or business groups, and connect with people in your industry. Building strong relationships with other business owners or professionals can lead to partnerships, referrals, or even mentorship.

Providing Exceptional Customer Service

Excellent customer service is one of the easiest ways to grow your client base. Be responsive, listen to your customers' needs, and go the extra mile to make them happy. Word of mouth is still one of the most powerful marketing tools, and great service turns customers into advocates for your business.

9. Scaling Your Business

As your business grows, you'll reach a point where you need to expand. Scaling a business isn't just about increasing revenue; it's about creating a structure that can handle the growth without compromising quality. Here's how to approach it:

When and How to Hire Employees

One of the first signs that it's time to scale is when you can't manage all the work by yourself. If you find that tasks are slipping through the cracks, it may be time to hire help. Start by outsourcing tasks like accounting or marketing before moving on to full-time employees. Hiring strategically will help you grow without overwhelming your resources.

Automating and Streamlining Operations

As your business grows, you'll need to streamline processes to save time and reduce manual labor. Automate repetitive tasks like sending invoices, scheduling appointments, or tracking inventory. Invest in software that can handle more complex operations as you scale, so you're not caught off guard by growing pains.

Expanding Your Product/Service Offerings

Another way to scale is by diversifying what you offer. Listen to your customers, what additional services or products could meet their needs? Expanding doesn't mean overcomplicating your business. Focus on complementary products or services that enhance your current offerings and appeal to your existing customer base.

Scaling your business is an exciting time, but it's also a critical period where strategic decisions need to be made. By managing your operations effectively, growing your client base, and knowing when and how to expand, you're setting your business up for long-term success. Keep your goals in sight, and stay flexible as your business evolves.

PART 4

Sustaining Long-Term Success

At this stage, you've put in the work to start your business, and things are moving forward. But the real challenge isn't just starting, it's making sure your business stays strong and continues to grow. This section is about managing your business for the long haul and keeping it profitable.

10. Financial Management and Profitability

As a business owner, one of your main goals is profitability. You want your business to make money, but to do that, you need to keep your finances in check. Here's how to manage your business finances wisely:

Budgeting and Cash Flow

Creating a budget isn't just for big companies; it's critical for small businesses too. Your budget helps you plan where your money goes and ensures you're spending wisely. Always keep an eye on your cash flow, the money coming in and going out. When cash flow is tight, even a profitable business can struggle. Make sure you have enough cash on hand to cover everyday expenses.

Maximizing Profits and Cutting Costs

Look for ways to increase revenue while cutting unnecessary costs. This doesn't mean lowering the quality of your products or services, but rather finding more efficient ways to operate. For instance, could you renegotiate supplier contracts or switch to more cost-effective tools? Every dollar saved adds to your profit.

Understanding Taxes and Compliance

Taxes can be confusing, but staying on top of them is essential to avoid trouble down the road. Consider working with a tax professional to make sure you're paying what you owe and taking advantage of any deductions. Additionally, stay informed about regulations in your industry to keep your business compliant.

11. Overcoming Common Business Challenges

Running a business has its ups and downs. Here's how to face the inevitable challenges that will come your way:

Managing Stress and Avoiding Burnout

As a business owner, you'll likely wear many hats, and the workload can get overwhelming. It's important to find ways to manage stress and avoid burnout. Take breaks, delegate tasks when possible, and don't hesitate to seek support when you need it.

Navigating Setbacks and Failures

Every business faces setbacks, whether it's a tough month for sales or an unexpected expense. The key is to not panic. Learn from your mistakes, adjust your strategies, and move forward. Remember, failure is part of the learning process for every entrepreneur.

Staying Adaptable in a Changing Market

The business landscape is constantly evolving, whether due to technology, competition, or customer preferences. Stay flexible and open to change. Keep an eye on industry trends and be ready to adapt. This can be the difference between surviving and thriving in business.

12. Planning for the Future

A successful business is one that doesn't just focus on today, but also plans for the future. Here's how to build for long-term growth:

Long-Term Growth Strategies

As your business becomes more stable, think about how you can grow further. This might include expanding your product or service offerings, entering new markets, or increasing your customer base. Growth doesn't have to be fast; it should be strategic and manageable.

Building a Sustainable Business Model

Sustainability isn't just about being environmentally conscious; it's about making sure your business model can last over time. Focus on creating repeat customers and delivering consistent value. A business that can operate smoothly without you always at the helm is one that can last for years.

Exit Strategies

Even if you love running your business, it's important to think about the future. What happens if you want to retire or sell the business? Have an exit strategy in mind, whether that means passing the business to a family member, merging with another company, or selling it. Having a plan ensures your hard work pays off, even when you're ready to step back.

Sustaining long-term success in your business requires continuous effort and smart decisions. With careful financial management, the right mindset to overcome challenges, and strategic planning for the future, you can build a business that not only thrives today but continues to grow in the years to come.

Remember, success doesn't happen overnight, but with persistence and the right approach, it's entirely within your reach.

CONCLUSION

Reflecting on Your Entrepreneurial Journey

Starting your own business is no small feat, and the fact that you've come this far shows your determination and courage. It's important to recognize that every successful entrepreneur starts as a beginner, just like you. The road to business ownership will have its ups and downs, but with the knowledge and strategies you've learned in this guide, you're better prepared to navigate it.

Take a moment to appreciate how far you've come, whether you're still in the planning phase or already seeing your first customers. Reflect on the lessons you've learned, the skills you've developed, and the small victories you've achieved. Each step brings you closer to building the business you've dreamed of.

Staying Motivated and Focused on Your Goals

As you move forward, motivation will be key to your success. Every business will face obstacles, from tight finances to difficult customers, and there will be moments when you may feel like giving up. But here's the thing: challenges are part of the journey. What sets successful business owners apart is their ability to stay focused on their goals, even when the road gets tough.

Remember why you started this business in the first place. Whether it's financial independence, the desire to create something meaningful, or simply the joy of being your own boss, keeping your "why" in mind will fuel your drive to push through difficulties. Set clear, realistic goals for yourself, and celebrate your progress along the way. Keep refining your business, learning from your experiences, and staying adaptable. Growth doesn't happen overnight, but with consistent effort, you will get there.

You will appreciate this words from me

It's easy to look at successful businesses and assume they have everything figured out from day one, but that's rarely the case. Behind every great business is a story of persistence, learning, and growth. Your business will be no different. Mistakes will happen, and things may not always go as planned, but every setback is an opportunity to improve and grow stronger.

The fact that you're taking the leap into self-employment already puts you ahead of the many people who only dream of starting their own business but never do. Trust the process, trust yourself, and remember that every successful business starts with someone like you, someone willing to learn, adapt, and never give up.

With the right mindset, tools, and commitment, your business can thrive and become something truly remarkable. You've got this! Keep going, and let your passion drive you toward the success you've envisioned.

BONUS

DONE FOR YOU- 6 BUSINESS IDEAS AND PLANS FOR BEGINNERS

Offline Business Ideas

1. Mobile Car Wash Service

Plan:

Step 1: Research Your Market – Understand who your customers are (busy professionals, car owners with limited time) and where they are located.

Step 2: Get the Necessary Equipment – Purchase essential car wash tools like a pressure washer, sponges, eco-friendly soap, and cleaning towels. Getting a space suitable for a start

Step 3: Set Your Pricing – Offer affordable packages for basic wash, waxing, or detailing.

Step 4: Promote Locally – Use flyers, local Facebook groups, or neighborhood apps to market your services. Consider offering discounts for first-time customers.

Step 5: Deliver Excellent Service – Focus on quality and building relationships. Offer to visit customers' homes or offices for convenience.

2. Personal Fitness Trainer

Plan:

Step: Get Certified – Obtain a fitness trainer certification from a reputable institution.

This work best if you are fit yourself or interested in fitness – this will help earn people trust in you – you can hold personal fitness journey challenge and encourage others to join you.

Step 2: Choose Your Niche – Specialize in areas like weight loss, bodybuilding, or senior fitness based on your strengths and interests.

Step 3: Build a Local Client Base – Offer free trial sessions at local gyms, community centers, or through referrals.

Step 4: Set Your Prices – Start with affordable rates, especially for group sessions or package deals.

- **Step 5: Keep Learning** – Stay updated on new fitness trends and techniques to provide more value to your clients.

3. Handmade Crafts and Gifts

Plan:

Step 1: Find Your Craft – Choose a craft you're passionate about, like handmade jewelry, candles, or personalized gifts.

Step 2: Source Materials – Start small by buying affordable supplies. Research wholesalers for materials as your business grows.

Step 3: Create Samples – Make a small batch of products to showcase your work. Focus on quality and unique designs.

Step 4: Sell Locally – Start selling at local markets, pop-up events, or through word of mouth. You can also partner with local stores to display your items.

Step 5: Scale Over Time – As demand increases, streamline your production and consider expanding online.

Online Business Ideas

1. Freelance Content Writing

Plan:

Step 1: Build a Portfolio – Start writing sample articles or blog posts in different niches like health, technology, or lifestyle.

Step 2: Find Clients – Use platforms like Upwork, Fiverr, or LinkedIn to find writing gigs. Start with small projects to gain experience and reviews.

Step 3: Set Your Rates – Offer competitive prices initially, then gradually increase as you gain more clients and experience.

Step 4: Market Yourself – Create a personal website or blog to showcase your writing. Use social media to attract potential clients.

Step 5: Expand Your Services – Offer related services like copywriting, SEO content, or email marketing to diversify your income.

2. Online Tutoring

Plan:

Step 1: Choose Your Subject – Pick a subject you are proficient in, whether it's math, language, or science.

Step 2: Set Up Tutoring Platforms – Register on tutoring platforms like Chegg, TutorMe, or VIPKid.

You can also offer tutoring independently using Zoom or Skype.

Step 3: Create a Curriculum – Prepare lesson plans and study materials based on the level of your students.

Step 4: Set Competitive Pricing – Offer a range of pricing options for one-on-one or group sessions. Consider offering a free trial or first lesson discount.

Step 5: Build a Reputation – Encourage students to leave reviews and referrals, which will help you attract more clients.

3. Drop-shipping Business

Plan:

Step 1: Choose a Niche – Find a product niche that has demand but isn't oversaturated (like eco-friendly products or home workout gear).

Step 2: Find a Supplier – Use dropshipping platforms like Shopify, Oberlo, or AliExpress to find reliable suppliers.

Step 3: Set Up an Online Store – Create a store on Shopify or WooCommerce. Ensure your site is user-friendly and visually appealing.

Step 4: Market Your Products – Run ads on Facebook, Instagram, and Google, and use influencer marketing to drive traffic to your store.

Step 5: Focus on Customer Service – Although you won't be handling inventory, it's important to maintain excellent communication with customers for returns, shipping, and inquiries.

THE END

www.ingramcontent.com/pod-product-compliance
Lightning Source LLC
Chambersburg PA
CBHW040339220526
45473CB00009B/2733